Headphones on Strike
Copyright © 2024 Jennifer Jones
All copyright laws and rights reserved.
Published in the U.S.A.
For more information, email info@ninjalifehacks.tv
Paperback ISBN: 978-1-63731-919-2
Hardcover ISBN: 978-1-63731-921-5
eBook ISBN: 978-1-63731-920-8

Find the Headphones on Strike lesson plans at ninjalifehacks.tv

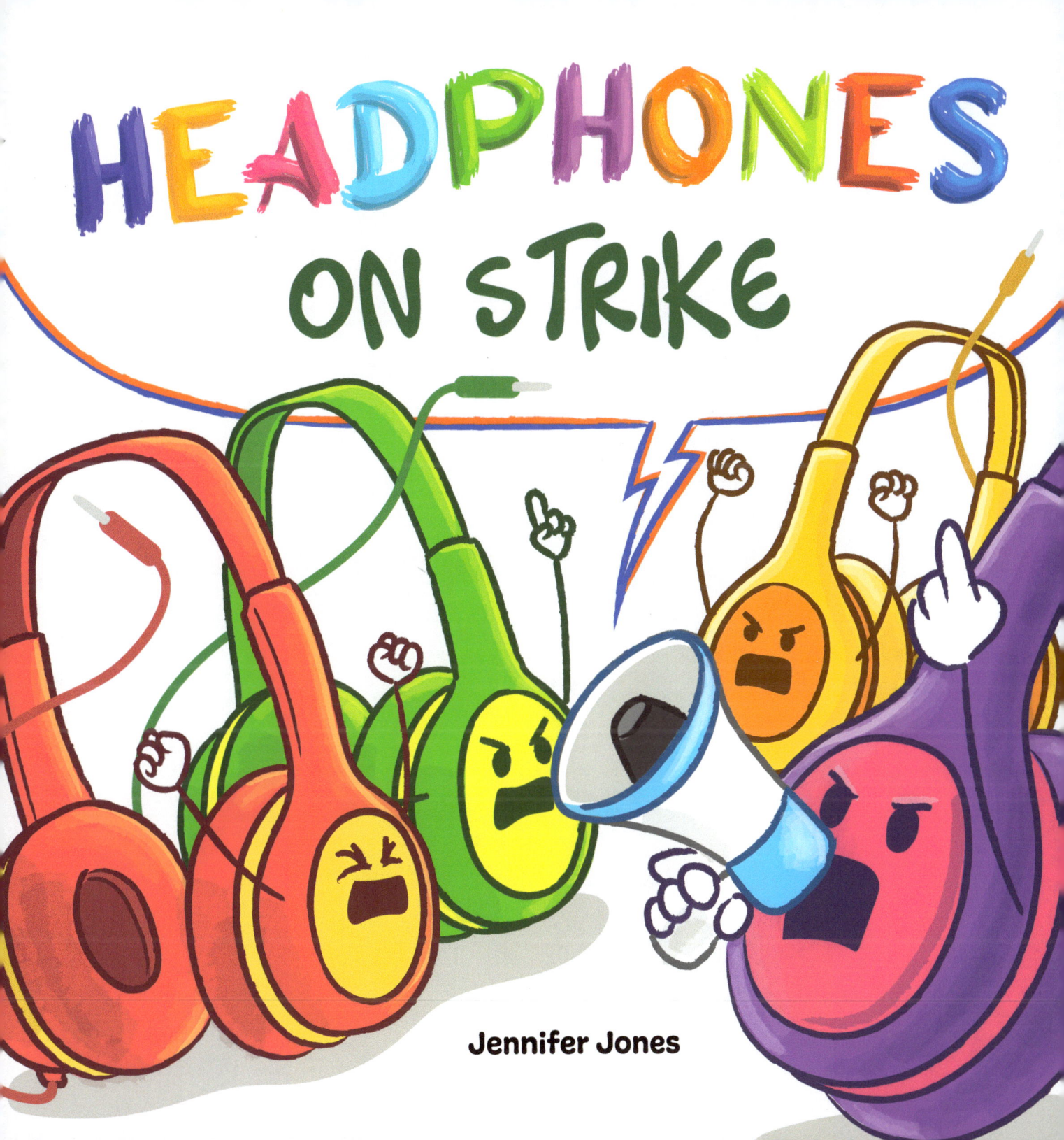

Far in the corner of the classroom,
some special school supplies stay.
They're the trusty classroom headphones,
but things aren't going their way.

So on that day, they made a decision.
They couldn't take it anymore.
They wrote the kids a letter
and hid away, that's for sure.

They found the note on the desk
and quickly began to frown.
Without their headphones, their work was tough.
They needed them to come back around.

www.ingramcontent.com/pod-product-compliance
Lightning Source LLC
Chambersburg PA
CBHW041653160426
43171CB00050B/92